بسم الله الرحمن الرحيم

DA'WA

ABDUSSABUR
KIRKE

This discourse is not subject to copyright.

Abdussabur Kirke asserts the moral right to be identified as its author.

Lifeboat Press

Contact: abdussabur.kirke@gmail.com

DA'WA

Discourse given
in Cambridge
14 July 2024

What we seek to get from reciting these awrad is partly for ourselves on our Path, but it is not just for yourself. We have to take the light of it out to the people of this country. It is absolutely obligatory, and imperative, that we see a twofold task of being in this country. We are here. Allah, subhanahu wa ta'ala, has put us here, whether we be of the place or we have come from another place – it makes no difference.

There is no ambition that is proper other than that the people of this country become Muslim. There is no other way of looking at it. If you want proof that this can happen, then go outside and walk around Cambridge and see all the churches of the Christians. They were not always there. That is the proof. If the Christians can make this country Christian, how can it be that we – however few we may be and whatever situation we may be in – cannot have that ambition for Islam? Especially now that Christianity is essentially gone.

We are permitted to have ambition for this, because the Messenger of Allah, sallallahu alayhi wa sallam, was ambitious in bringing Allah's Word out to mankind. He sent his people out in delegations to places near and far. He himself went out.

This is our job. This is the reason we are here. We may be here for our work or for family reasons – this does not contradict that. Allah has placed you among people. Especially in a town like this, you are placed among the elite of this whole society. You must take this message of what we have been reciting here, and what you yourselves have, and find a way to articulate it to the people with whom you mingle.

There are as many ways of articulating it – calling people to Allah – as there are Muslims. There is not one way. For example, we recited Surat al-Waqi'a, which everyone is familiar with, and it contains one thing that you can say to anyone who asks: "What is this thing that you believe in?" We believe that Allah ta'ala will classify all people into three. In the beginning of Surat al-Waqi'a:

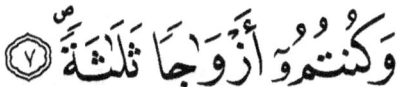

And you will be classed into three.

What this means is, every single human being is going to fall into one of those three categories: the People of the Right, the People of the Left and the Sabiqun, the Forerunners. So that is part of the Message that you have to convey.

Or, you could relate to someone who is a

reflective individual the words of the qasida we have just recited in which Shaykh Muhammad ibn al-Habib says that "created beings are nothing but meanings set up in forms." Creation, of course, means things: physical, inanimate things but also animate things. So he is saying that stuff – and we ourselves – are nothing other than meanings in manifest form. This is something that the people out there are going to be willing to think about. People are waiting to hear this, because they have absolutely no other message that makes sense. There is nothing being said to them which will untie the knot for them, except from what we have.

But you have to find the way to say it and you have to find the right moment. You have to gauge the moment and the right words. Some individuals find it very easy to say these things straight out. They can just speak out in front of anybody. It is what Allah has given them. Some people cannot do that; they cannot bring themselves to do it, but if that is the case, Allah will nevertheless give you another way of conveying it, whether it be by what you say openly, or what you say or ask for inside yourself.

But I say to you: the condition for calling people to Islam is not a lot of knowledge. It is not having masses of knowledge, or waiting until you know the right words. It is courage. It is courage. How do you acquire courage? You acquire courage by doing the thing before you are ready. You can never wait until the perfect circumstances arrive, because the world is, in its worldliness, imperfect. You will never be 'ready' to carry this message, but you must carry it. And then Allah, subhanahu wa ta'ala, will teach you. From doing this, you will get knowledge and abilities which you never knew you could even have.

So this calling people to Islam is half of what we have to do. And what we do in these gatherings of dhikr, in a way, is just preparing ourselves to be in the right condition to go out, to be in a condition which makes the tongue loose with the Words of Allah, whereas before it was tied up. And it makes the heart open, whereas before it was closed up – because that is in fact what it is all about. It is not really about knowing the intellectual argument. It is about something else.

The other half of what we have to do here in this place, England – because this is where we are – is to help the Muslims. We have to help the non-Muslims by calling them onto the lifeboat of Islam, and we have to help the Muslims in a different way. This is what we have to do. The path of this Tasawwuf which we are on is actually a path of outward action. Many of the things that we are commanded to do in Qur'an are feeding the poor, helping the orphan, visiting the sick; and doing the Prayer of course, but *aqimu*-Salat: *establish* the Prayer. Don't just do it yourself. You have to 'set it on its feet' – which means, for men, publicly. This brings us back to Da'wa. Go out and do it in the parks, in groups. Not just at Eids. People will see. And they will not forget what they see. We were here in Cambridge the other day and a few of us did the Prayer in a park full of people because the time had come upon us, and the people near us immediately started asking, "What is it you're doing? How many Prayers do you have to do? When's your last Prayer in the day?" This praying in public opens a conversation.

It's like the man who just now had been listening at the window for ten minutes because he liked the sound of the singing. He was British. He loved what he heard and wanted to come in, but maybe he was too shy. You know, the existence of all the indigenous Muslim community of Spain comes from three men walking through London, passing a house, and hearing what we were just now reciting. They listened through the letterbox, then they came back the next day to listen again, and eventually they plucked up the courage to knock on the door. They all quickly became Muslims, and ultimately, from that, came the Great Mosque of Granada, and will come the Great Mosque of Seville, inshallah. And all the second and third generation of Spanish Muslims – all from that exact same thing that just happened here now.

You also have to realise the depth of nothingness that the people out there are in. They are desperate to know. Because everybody is created as a potential knower of their Lord. Not everybody will get there. Allah ta'ala is not going to save everybody. But everybody was told in the beginning and affirmed what they are, and so you have to remind them. You will do it especially in groups going out – twos and threes. I love it how here in the airports and motorway service stations and hospitals there are musallahs and prayer rooms springing up where people who don't know each other pray together. It's the most wonderful thing. And people with the means must establish more of these kinds of places. Also in the universities.

Everybody has a role they can play. For some people it is a quiet role. For some people it is an open role. There is a lot to do. What we do, taken to its highest dimension, drives you out of the house to be among the people and makes you say, "I want to take this up. I want to be on the front line of this." We need to take this to people. We are in this country and it is not for no reason. Allah says in Qur'an:

Our Lord,
You have not created this for nothing.

This means the physical creation, but it also means the creation of your actions and your destiny of where you have arrived. It is not for nothing that you have arrived at where you are. You are in exactly the place you are in for Allah's reason. This may be hidden within the worldly reason; it goes in the vehicle of your worldly reason. It may drive in the world of *I'm here for a job* – and that is perfectly legitimate – but inside the vehicle is the real meaning, which is that somehow the moment will come when you can say something. If you cannot say something, say something anyway. Even Musa, alayhi salam, asked Allah:

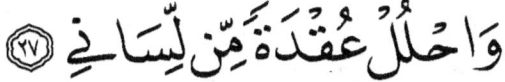

And loosen the knot in my tongue.

So if Musa, alayhi salam, who was a Messenger of Allah, can struggle to find the words, there is nothing wrong with us struggling.

This is what we have to do, and it is a joyous task which also our children inshallah will inherit from us. It is not to do with knowing a lot of things. It is to do with what condition you are in and having courage and seeing what situation Allah has put you in and what He has given you, subhanahu wa ta'ala – what tools he has given you with the particular form you have got. You have within reach of your hand what you need.

This is what we seek to remember when we do this dhikr. It is a very simple thing and it excludes nobody. In this regard there is no 'imam class' of people who are above the other and to whom we delegate this duty. Allah will put His Light wherever He wants, subhanahu wa ta'ala. In fact, the moment you think, "Oh, I've got something, I have become something," then you will find someone far ahead of you. We are permitted to compete on that basis, but the competing of the Sufi is counter-intuitive, because rather than saying to itself, "I am better," it says "He is better." It puts the other person forward and forgets about itself in seeing the other, to the extent that the person doesn't see anything but better people among the Muslims – not in a despairing way about yourself, but in a way that sees good without end among the Muslims.

That is arriving at something interesting. This knowledge and this Path are not about having a position or a certain kind of persona. They are actually about abandoning persona.

We ask Allah, subhanahu wa ta'ala, to give us – every one of us – a means of talking about Him and His Messenger, sallallahu alayhi wa sallam, and if we cannot talk, then a means of showing it. We ask Allah, subhanahu wa ta'ala, to keep us together with the Muslims at all times, protect us from our aloneness, protect us from being lost among people who do not believe in anything, and if we have to be among them, then bring us swiftly back to people of iman in Allah and his Messenger, sallallahu alayhi wa sallam.

Allah, bless this household with a blessing that never finishes. Allah, bring angels with us which never depart, protect the householder and all of the people who have come here from this town. Allah, bless the Cambridge Muslim College, and bless Yaseen in his role there and give him enormous success, and to all those who have set that place up, and the Mosque here – protect it and expand it and only give it increase and bring new Muslims to this city by means of it. Also make Islam come to life in the hospitals and in the university. Allah put us among the best of people so that we may have the efficiency of talking to those who will convey it on to others after we are gone.

We ask Allah, subhanahu wa ta'ala, to give us a good seal. Make us arrive at the end with Your Name on our lips, celebrating in Your Nearness and in what is to come.

Fatiha.

www.ingramcontent.com/pod-product-compliance
Lightning Source LLC
Chambersburg PA
CBHW072024290426
44109CB00018B/2332